Wealth Management Path

How to manage your finances to achieve
your financial goals successful

ROBERTS KENNY

All rights reserved

No part of this publication can be reproduced,stored in a retrieval system in any form,or by any means mechanical,electronic, photocopying,print or otherwise,without permission in writing from the publisher.

COPYRIGHT © 2024 BY ROBERTS KENNY

Table of contents

Introduction

Wealth management is a comprehensive service that focuses on taking a holistic view of a client's financial situation and includes services such as investment management, financial planning, tax planning, legal and estate planning. Such services are provided by financial services companies or recognized specialists such as: CFP (Certified Financial Planner), CPA (Certified Public Accountant), CFA (Chartered Financial Analyst) for high net worth individuals. The booming economy and associated rise in income levels have increased demand for wealth management services. The huge amounts of money these people make must be handled carefully. This is the reason why wealth management is becoming a highly sought-after service in the United States, Europe and India.

Chapter One

How does asset management work

In simple terms, wealth management is a form of financial advice for companies and individuals to properly manage their financial affairs. These could include:

- Investment management and advice.
- Comprehensive financial planning
- Tax planning and accounting services.
- Estate planning
- Philanthropic planning
- Legal advice
- Retirement planning

Specifically, asset management strategies involve preserving funds for the long term. The process is usually as follows:

The first and most important step for the wealth manager is to determine his or her financial objectives, risk tolerance, and investment horizon.

In the second step, he/she will develop a strategic plan for you. This step involves suggesting appropriate strategies, taking into account your current tax obligations, liquidity concerns, and past and current investments.

The asset manager then executes the plan. Your money is invested in a preferred financial instrument and the asset manager implements your investment strategy.

The final step is for your wealth manager to make changes and subsequent evaluations to your plan as your needs and preferences change.

•What are the characteristics of asset management?

As mentioned above, those with significant net worth prefer wealth management services. Many HNWIs have complicated assets abroad, which is why they need to seek such professional services.

However, here are some specifics to asset management:

It is a personalized service and adapted specifically to the client. Therefore, investment strategies and products are suggested based on your preferences. A wealth manager carefully considers your risk tolerance, investment horizon, liabilities, and assets before making a decision.

The work of an asset manager goes far beyond financial advice. Instead, they offer several other services such as: How to find ways to create more wealth, periodically review your plans and more.

This service also takes into account various aspects to balance the financial needs of your family. The tasks an asset manager performs in this context include retirement planning,tax management, insurance planning and more.

•What are the objectives of asset management?

Asset management is an advisory process. This also includes advising clients to discuss their financial goals.

The main objectives of wealth management services for individuals and companies include:

•Venture capital investment
•Hedge derivatives
•Real estate planning
•Stock option planning

What are the wealth management strategies?

Asset management involves much more than just financial planning. It takes care of all other financial aspects of high net worth individuals.

However, below are some strategies that asset managers follow:

1. Risk analysis

Risk analysis involves assessing a client's ability to tolerate risk in relation to her finances. Factors that determine this include the investment objective, the client's personality, future and current responsibilities, and more. A wealth manager considers these and many other factors to clearly understand a client's risk tolerance.

2. Division of assets

The asset allocation step involves creating an appropriate allocation plan to ensure applicability to the client's risk-reward needs. This maximizes investment return while the asset manager manages the overall risk of the portfolio.

3. Selection of investment products

Asset managers in the US, Europe and India work closely with leading banks ensuring the availability of various investment instruments. However, asset managers often seek to uncover specialized investment opportunities that go beyond these opportunities. These special instruments vary from customer to customer and can be customized.

4. Execution of the plan and research.
A money manager also closely monitors the performance of various investments. In most cases, clients receive ongoing qualitative and quantitative reports that indicate whether the portfolio is being executed correctly. This is an important strategy considering that investing involves risk.

•What are the benefits of asset management?
The high net worth segment in the US, Europe and India is growing rapidly, leading

to increasing demand for wealth management services. These services offer a variety of benefits including:

1. Provides a systematic financial plan.
When you use a wealth management service, the advisor will help you create a strategic financial plan. With the right advice, you can systematically build wealth over the long term. In this way, wealth management services help formulate a systematic financial plan.

2. Eliminate financial stress
Through their knowledge and experience, asset managers help their clients understand financial uncertainty. They also help you make critical decisions when the time comes. In this way, they help people make financial decisions even in fluctuating market conditions. This leads to less stress and better financial decisions.

3. Expand a flexible investment strategy

Asset managers continually develop investment strategies for the benefit of their clients. Therefore, they offer a flexible financial approach according to your financial needs and requirements. An asset manager takes into account market conditions and categories at the same time. This helps them chart a path through the market's ups and downs, leading to better investment decisions.

Chapter Two

The basics of personal finance

Personal finances can seem very intimidating; After all, they encompass every decision you make with your money throughout your life. it doesn't have to be complicated! You can trust me.

When you break it down, you'll discover that the basics of personal finance are actually very manageable steps that you can and will master. Then let's get started.

•Create a budget
First, you need to create a budget. Because? Budgeting is the foundation on which all other personal finance habits are built. That's because budgeting simply

means making a plan for your money: every dollar that comes in and every dollar that goes out. Here you will find out how this works.

First, list your income. Income is any money you plan to receive this month. This includes net salary and any additional funds.
Then, subtract all your expenses. Start by giving and saving, then plan your four walls: food, supplies, shelter, and transportation. Next, list your typical monthly expenses, such as insurance and childcare. If you still have money left, list additional services like dining out and entertainment.
If you still have money left after deducting all expenses, give them a high five. But don't leave this money as "extra." Use it to achieve your current monetary goal e.g save or pay off debts.

If you end up with a negative number, you must reduce spending until your income minus your expenses is zero.

The next step in budgeting is this: track your spending (which, by the way, is one of our top personal finance tips, period). Do it throughout the month. This means that any money that goes into or out of your bank account must be recorded in your budget, on the correct budget line.

This will help you stay on top of your spending, prevent you from overspending, and be realistic about your financial habits. Because your budget is the plan and follow-up is the responsibility.

Finally, create a new budget each month (before the month starts). Remember to take into account all of your specific expenses for the month so you're prepared for what's ahead.

•Save for large purchases or semi-annual expenses

Not all of your life expenses are regular monthly expenses. You should use a sinking fund to save over time, like when your car tires start to wear out: start saving for replacements.

You have an insurance premium that is due twice a year – split the cost and save a portion of the total each month.

You have an annual membership to something; again, split the cost and save something each month.

If you want to repair your house or buy new furniture, save until you can pay the full amount.

A sinking fund is a great way to save for large, semi-annual expenses because you can budget them over time to spread out the costs. This way, your budget won't be surprised by something you knew was coming.

•Build an emergency fund
Your grandmother told you to save for a rainy day. Because why? It will Rain. She called it a rainy day fund; We call it an emergency fund.

Start with an initial fund of $1,000. Then, once you've paid off all your debt (more on this later), use the extra money you spent paying off debt to build your fully funded emergency fund. Here is how.

First, look at your budget. How much does it cost to keep your home running each month? What essential bills and obligations would you still have to pay if your income stopped?

You want to save enough to cover three to six months of these expenses in case of an emergency. (That's three months if you have a two-income household and six months if you have a single income.)

Keep this money liquid, i.e make sure it is available. Your emergency fund is not a long-term investment, but rather an insurance policy. And it has to be ready when you need it. But that doesn't mean you put it between the mattress and the box spring. (That's too available.)

Instead, keep the money in a basic money market account so you can access it by writing a check or going to an ATM. That way, it won't be a temptation to sit with your usual money as the summer holidays approach. (This is not an emergency, to be clear, no matter how much you crave the salt air.)

With your emergency fund fully stocked, you'll be prepared for whatever comes your way. This type of personal financial security will help you rest better than a nap by the sea.

•Save for retirement
Investing for retirement isn't as complicated as you might think. First, let's talk about how much you should invest. If you follow the Baby Steps, you'll start setting aside 15% of your income for

retirement once you've paid off all your debt and saved up that fully funded emergency fund we just talked about.

If you've reached this point, here's what you should do: See if your employer offers a 401(k) or 403(b) with a match. If this is the case, invest in your 401(k) balance until you match with the employer to take advantage of this free money.

If you already have a traditional 401(k) through work (that is, you fund it with pre-tax dollars), the next step is to open a Roth IRA, which you fund with after-tax dollars to support your growth and enable your withdrawals later to be tax free!

But because the Roth gives you such a big tax advantage, Uncle Sam sets a limit: You can only invest $6,500 in 2024 (or $7,500 if you're 50 or older). If you max out and haven't reached 15% yet, go back to your 401(k) and continue investing your money there.

With both the 401(k) and the Roth IRA, he wants his money to be spread across the four types of mutual funds: growth, growth and income, aggressive growth, and international.

This way you won't invest all your savings in one basket.This is what the investment world calls diversification, and it's less risky and just plain smart.

•Get the right insurance
Insurance is a lot of fun, right? Well, maybe not for most of us.that doesn't mean it's not important. And maybe you know that you should get insurance, but you don't really know what type, or how much, or with whom.

Don't worry. Here's a super quick overview of the eight types of insurance you need:

Term Life Insurance: Life insurance is about the protection and security of your family. You need term life insurance with a duration of 15 or 20 years. Average term life insurance rates are typically cheaper than life insurance rates. Additionally, term life insurance is not a total scam like life insurance, which looks like an investment policy but has terrible returns.

Car Insurance: In general, to get the most sensible car insurance, you need comprehensive insurance, including liability, collision, and comprehensive. If you have an old, depreciated car, you may want to think about avoiding a collision. There are several other optional types and other add-ons that your state may require you to purchase. It's a good idea to talk to an independent insurance broker to discuss your options and get the best rates.

Homeowner's or renter's insurance: If you're a homeowner, make sure you have expanded home coverage and talk to your insurance agent about flood and earthquake coverage. Dear Tenants: Your landlord is not responsible for replacing your belongings if they are lost in a fire, theft, or other disaster. That's why you need renters insurance to cover the cost of replacing your belongings!

Health Insurance: A major medical emergency can literally ruin you if you don't have health insurance. However, if you're concerned about costs, consider high-deductible health insurance combined with a health savings account (HSA). This is a great way to protect yourself in an emergency without paying an incredibly high premium each month.

Long-term disability insurance: Get long-term disability insurance to help replace your income if you can no longer work due to illness or injury. We recommend insuring as much as possible: around 60-70% of your income. You don't need a short-term disability. (Your fully funded emergency fund has you covered.)

Long-term care insurance: If you need long-term care in your golden years, you can't expect Medicare to take care of you. So when you turn 60, plan to purchase long-term care insurance that covers home care (not just nursing home care).

Identity Theft Protection: Listen. Identity theft can happen to anyone and can take years to resolve on your own. You need protection against identity theft! Make sure you get a plan that offers protection and recovery services. You need Social Security number monitoring, address change monitoring, recovery services and refunds.

That means someone else will put in all those hours to get your life back when you need it!

Umbrella Insurance: If your net worth exceeds $500,000, you need umbrella insurance to protect your home and savings from liability claims that go beyond your home and auto insurance coverage. It's not fun to think about, but it's necessary!

Ugh, that's a lot. But don't worry: you don't need to be an insurance expert to be well insured. (Thank God!)

•Personal Finance Basics
Get a will
We'll just come out and say it: you need a will. It's part of getting your finances in order and being a responsible adult; It's not fun, but it's an important part.

You don't want the government to decide what happens to your stuff, your money, or your family (which is exactly what will happen if you don't take responsibility here).

 Yes, there is a lot to deal with: making important decisions about something you don't even want to think about. But listen, you need a will.
   Find an affordable, verified online provider that cuts through the legal jargon and simplifies the process. (By "easy" we mean you can easily do the paperwork in your pajamas.) So don't hesitate. Get a will today.

   •Pay your debts
   Some people think of debt as a tool to build credit or earn big airline miles.The truth is that debt is a burden that overwhelms you and holds you back. Research shows that one in five Americans have fallen further into debt since June 2022 and only 24% said they have reduced their debt.

Unfortunately, debt and stress work hand in hand. This could be because debt is preventing you from moving forward. It holds part of your salary hostage each month with payments for something you bought months or even years ago. You don't need that kind of stress!

Here's an extremely important personal finance tip: Your income is your most important tool for building wealth. When you pay your debt, you get your paycheck back. You will receive back any additional payments you made to pay off the debt.

What do you do with that extra cash? Use it to get additional flexibility in your budget. Use it to advance your money goals, like savings and retirement!

In short, debt is not a tool. Your income is.Take it back.

•Make smart housing decisions

We could make this really complicated. But that's not our thing. Our goal is to make personal finance clear and simple.

These are the three most important points to consider when thinking about buying a home.

Spend no more than 25% of your net monthly income on housing costs. If you're getting a mortgage, that means your monthly payment, PMI, property taxes, insurance, and any HOA fees combined should be no more than 25%. (The same rule applies to renters: rent and any other associated fees must not exceed 25%).

If you want to take out a mortgage, choose a conventional loan with a fixed interest rate and a term of 15 years. (You'll save literally thousands of dollars total compared to expensive FHA, VA, and 30-year loans.)

Save at least 20% of the cost of the home for a down payment to avoid PMI fees before purchasing a home. (First-time buyers can save a smaller down payment, like 5 to 10%, but then they'll be stuck with PMI.)

If you don't follow these three guidelines, you can quickly find yourself in poverty. This means that while your house is great, it consumes such a large portion of your income that you are struggling financially in other areas.

•Get a game plan for your money

So, yes, personal finances are a lot. But you can make better decisions with your money, whether big or small.You just need the right game plan.

Chapter Three

Cash inflows and outflows

•What are cash inflows and outflows?

Cash inflow is the money that comes into a company and can come from sales, investments or financing. It is the opposite of cash outflow, that is, money leaving the company. Knowing how to calculate and analyze both will help you make more informed strategic decisions and make the most of your limited resources.

•What is the difference between cash in and cash out?

This key figure provides a quick overview of cash inflows and outflows. Cash inflow is the money that comes into a company and can come from sales, investments or financing. It is the opposite of cash outflow, that is, money that leaves the company.

A company's ability to create shareholder value is determined by its ability to generate positive cash flows. This is an essential metric for assessing business health, especially when broken down into more granular categories such as operating expenses, capital expenses and debt.

Examples of cash inflows and outflows
Examples of cash inflows include income from the sale of products and income from investments. While, the cash outflow may consist of operating expenses, debt, and other liabilities.

•Why are cash inflows and outflows important?
Cash inflows and outflows represent the basic financial situation of your company.
Since cash is the lifeblood of any business, understanding your cash inflows

and outflows is essential for operational financing and managing daily activities.

•Interpreting cash flow

To build a business that can generate long-term profits, you need to know that your inputs will eventually exceed your outputs. When more money comes into your business than it goes out, it is said to have positive cash flow. Conversely, a negative cash flow means there are more outflows than inflows.

If you have positive cash flow, it is a good indicator that you have enough cash to invest in growing the business and pay shareholders without taking on excessive debt. This is critical for mature venture capital-backed startups and public companies that need to prove they can operate efficiently while growing.

Negative cash flow, on the other hand, means you spend more money than you earn.This is usually the norm for startups that want to grow at all costs. For this reason, a comprehensive view of cash inflows and outflows is not enough. What you really want is to drill down into the breakdown of cash inflows and outflows so you can continually improve efficiency and design more strategic growth plans.

More established businesses may be content with viewing cash flow statements monthly and quarterly. But for high-growth companies focused on maximizing their runway and maximizing the expansion of venture capital funds, cash flow analysis is typically more common.

More established companies may be able to prepare a cash flow statement once quarterly, but this is not the same for limited-term, higher-share startups.

Streamline your month-end financial closing process with this comprehensive checklist.

•Factors affecting cash flow
Since cash affects every aspect of your business, it makes sense that several factors can affect your cash flow.

Some business functions that has direct impact on cash flow:

•Account Receivable. Too many outstanding accounts receivable can slow the flow of money through your business and have a negative impact on cash flow. It's important to closely monitor accounts receivable metrics so you can identify overdue payments and quickly find a solution.
•Accounts Payable (AP). Paying suppliers on time contributes to smooth cash flow. However, if you have poor accounts payable management, late payment fees can

accumulate and damage supplier relationships, making it difficult to negotiate better purchasing terms.

•Number of employees. Headcount is the biggest cost for any SaaS company. As your business grows, you'll need to plan for a payroll that will significantly exceed any other cash outflows you need to manage.

•The cost of sales. Increasing sales and marketing costs is critical to achieving significant revenue goals. In the short term, the amount you spend on advertising will affect your cash flow. However, your cash flow analysis should also include long-term projections of how these ads translate into revenue.

SaaS pricing and cost of sales. SaaS pricing strategy isn't a perfect science, but you should price your products and services to optimize cash flow.

•Ways of Improving your Business Cash Flow

Improving cash flow can mean increasing positive cash flow or turning negative cash flow into positive one. To do this, you need to increase cash inflows, reduce cash outflows, or both.

These are some of the top strategic financial tactics you can use to improve your business's cash flow and unlock more resources for growth.

1. Rent instead of buy
Buying real estate and equipment may be cheaper in the long run, but requires more capital up front. Even if you finance your purchase, many banks and lenders require a 20% to 30% down payment.

This may not be a deal breaker for more established businesses, but many small businesses and startups need to be very strategic with their cash flow when starting out.

When you lease, you get the same equipment at a lower initial cost and can negotiate terms to reduce your monthly expenses. This reduces your cash outflow and leaves more money in your business that you can use for operating expenses.

Modern CEOs and finance departments should consider cash flow and bottom line savings when setting their budgets.

2. Create incentives for early and punctual payments

Late customer payments can put pressure on your cash flow. Your suppliers won't extend your payment dates just because you're waiting on your accounts receivable.

If your customers don't always pay on time, you need to change your payment terms. Try offering discounts for early payment or including clauses in your contracts that penalize late payments.

3. Improve accounts receivable processes

In addition to changing your terms, review your billing procedures and see if there are any payment barriers you can address. In particular, be sure to send invoices promptly and give your clients enough time to review and pay them.

Finally, accepting online forms of payment, such as credit, debit, and ACH deposits, can reduce late payments associated with mailing checks. SaaS companies can benefit from setting up recurring payments to avoid chasing customers and reminding them about payments.

4. Adjust your cash flow forecasts.

When forecasting cash flow you can make use of your existing cash flow to predict your future bank balance.
When managing a startup's finances, you need to approach cash flow forecasting differently.

For example, you should focus on both short-term and long-term cash flow. With short-term cash flow reports, you can see how you manage your limited runway in real time. With Mosaic, you can easily access this information from your financial dashboard.

Cash Flow Analysis Dashboard
Mosaic Cash Flow Analysis Template
CEOs and CFOs must play an active role in monitoring cash flow trends so they can improve money management and optimize their limited resources. In this way, cash flow becomes a future-oriented strategic tool and not simply another element of ex post financial analysis.

5. Pay suppliers electronically
Same-day transactions are better for your cash flow, especially in your accounts payable department. It's better to know that your account will be charged the same day you make the payment rather than waiting

for your provider to clear the check after receiving it in the mail.

Use credit and debit payments for your expenses to improve your overall financial efficiency. As an added bonus, you may be able to take advantage of early payment discounts, reduce late payment fees, and even receive cash rewards from your credit card provider.

And if you are known as a customer who always pays on time, you have the opportunity to negotiate better terms with your suppliers.

6. Adjust your pricing strategy
Sometimes you've done everything you can to reduce expenses, but you can't achieve positive cash flow or you don't have enough money available to invest in growth.

In this case, it may be time to rethink your pricing strategy. This may mean raising prices or charging fees for features and services you provided for free.

According to CB Insights,15% of startups fail due to pricing or cost issues. That may not seem like much until you realize that bad pricing kills more startups than bad teams, bad timing, and inferior products.

It may be tempting to stick with freemium models to help with customer acquisition, but if you want to grow your business, you need to be able to charge based on the value you offer.

When it comes to improving cash inflows and outflows, the most important thing is visibility
Running a business without reviewing finances is like a doctor trying to select a treatment without taking his patient's vital signs.

CEOs and CFOs who understand company cash flow are critical for startups, small businesses, and corporations alike. Figuring out how money comes in and out of your business can make the difference between getting another round of funding or giving up.

Chapter four

SmartAsset: Definition and calculation of liquid net assets

When evaluating your short- and long-term financial goals, it can be helpful to compare the value of your assets with that of your liabilities.This is where net worth comes into play; Ultimately, this value can help you decide whether you should reduce your monthly expenses, set up a retirement account, or adjust your tax withholdings. The two main types of net worth are total net worth and liquid net worth. If you want to increase your wealth, a financial advisor is the best professional who can help you by creating a financial plan and helping you manage your investments.

Liquid assets: definition

Net worth is the money you have in cash or cash equivalents after you subtract your liabilities from your liquid assets. It is quite similar to net worth, but the only difference is that it does not take into account illiquid assets such as real estate or retirement accounts.

However, your total net worth is influenced by both liquid and illiquid assets.This means you must add up the value of all your assets, including vehicles, real estate, retirement accounts, securities, cash, and anything else of monetary value. You then deduct the value of your obligations from this sum. you'll have negative net worth if your liabilities exceed your assets. You have positive net worth if your assets have a greater monetary value than your liabilities.

Liabilities are financial debts that must be paid.This may include student loans, car loans, credit card balances, taxes, or mortgages. The liabilities of a business you own should not be included in your personal net worth.

•What are liquid assets in detail?
Liquid assets are cash or assets that can be easily converted into cash.

Examples of liquid assets include cash, savings accounts and checking accounts. Although there is some debate about this, some people also consider liquid accounts receivable, stocks, mutual funds, bonds, and any other securities that can be quickly converted into cash.

There are two key metrics for measuring liquid assets, both commonly used by companies but also applicable to individuals. One of them is the quick ratio. It measures how well a company can meet its short-term obligations (e.g debt payments, payroll, inventory costs, etc.) with its cash balance.

In this case, "cash" is defined as actual cash or cash-like assets that can be quickly converted. Cash-like assets are traditionally defined as liquid assets that the company can easily sell, such as: stocks or short-term income, such as Accounts receivable pending collection. These are the company's "quick" assets, which give the quick ratio its name. The quick ratio is then defined as the ratio of all liabilities due within the next year to all cash or income due within the next year.

Another reason is the current ratio. It compares a company's current assets with the debts it must pay during the year. It is calculated by simply dividing a company's total assets (cash and easily convertible assets) by its current liabilities (trade payables for the year). Once you have calculated the current ratio, you can draw conclusions about the company.

•How is liquid net worth calculated?
    You can determine your liquid net worth by subtracting the total amount of your liabilities from the total amount of your liquid assets. However, some liquid assets may have a liquidity discount, so you should take this into account when calculating your final liquid net worth.

    For example, let's say you have $20,000 in cash, $150,000 in brokerage accounts, and $101,000 in a 401(k) account. If these are your only liquid assets, your total liquid assets are $271,000. If you only owe $5,000 in credit card debt and $42,000 in student loans, your total debt would be $47,000. Minus that from $271,000 and your liquid net worth will be $224,000.

Chapter five

How to Create a Budget: Your Step-by-Step Guide

Creating a budget may seem overwhelming at first, but hear this: you can do it.by breaking down the process a little. No one actually eats an elephant by swallowing it at once (Takes one bite at a time). And no one dives into budgeting like a pro. (You go step by step).

So, let's start: little by little, step by step. How to create a budget in a few five steps.

- List your income
- List your expenses
- Deduct expenses from income
- Track your transactions

•Before the start of the month create a new budget

What is a budget?
But let's define the word "budget" very quickly. A budget is just a plan. This is not a spending limit, but rather a plan for what you do with your money. It's a plan for what comes in and what goes out.

When you learn to create a budget, each month, you give meaning to your money. You take control. Goodbye money anxiety. Hello, money goals.

Read on to learn how to make this happen so you can create a budget that works for you.

•Five steps on how to create a budget
No matter how you feel about budgeting, your financial goals, or your income, you can create and maintain a budget in just five steps.

First, decide whether you will create a budget on paper, in a spreadsheet, or in an app. (We know a great tool called EveryDollar. Just sayin'.) In any case, it's perfectly fine to start by writing everything down on a piece of paper.

Before we dive into the individual steps, open your online bank account or get your bank statements. This will give you the information you need when you start crunching your budget numbers.

Step 1: List your income
Income is all the money you plan to earn this month; That is, your regular salary and any extra money you make from a part-time job, garage sale, freelancing or similar.

Do you work as a barista or bagpiper on loan on weekends? This is income and goes into your budget.

Create separate income budget lines for each paycheck you (and your spouse) earn, as well as any additional income. Note: You're working with net income here, which is what you bring in after taxes or anything else deducted from your paycheck. Here is an example:

Your salary 1: $1,500
Your paycheck 1: $1,500
Your salary 2: $1,500
Your paycheck 2: $1,500
Secondary activity: $500
Total income: $6,500

If your income is irregular, look at what you've earned in recent months and put the lowest amount as your planned income budget line for this month. You can make adjustments later in the month if you earn more and add the extra money to your monetary goal or another budget line.

Step 2: List your expenses

Now that you have planned the money coming in, you can plan the money going out. It's time to list your expenses! (Yes, then the bank account or bank statement is very useful).

When you create a budget, set aside money for donations before entering all the things you'll pay for this month. We believe in 10% of your income here and we are always generous! Next, set a budget for your savings goals, such as an emergency fund (depending on your small step, which we'll talk more about in a moment). You have to pay yourself first before you pay others!

What's Next?
Cover your four walls. These are food, supplies, accommodation and transportation. Create a budget category for each of these and create budget lines below for your specific expenses.

Think of a budget category as a folder and the rows as the files it contains. Or the category is like a playlist and the lines are like the songs. Either It's okay, you understand.

Budget Category: Food
Groceries: $400

Budget Category: Utilities
Electricity: $75
Water: $50
Natural gas: $20

Budget category: Accommodation/Lodging
Mortgage: $1,500
Homeowners Association Fees: $50

Budget category: transportation
Gasoline: $200

Some of these are called fixed costs: expenses that stay the same every month, such as: Your rent or mortgage.

Other expenses such as groceries or changing gasoline. By the way, the household food budget is very difficult to guess at first glance, so start with a really good estimate based on your past expenses. You'll find out more about what you really need here in the coming months.

Next, list all other monthly expenses. Start with the essentials: we're talking insurance, debt, child care, etc. Then work on a section with miscellaneous and all non-essential items such as personal expenses, money for fun and entertainment.

Then use your online bank account or these statements to estimate how much you want to spend on everything.

Here's a quick note. If you're working to save money, get out of debt, or pursue another financial goal, you'll reach your goal much faster if you cut back on non-essential spending.

Create new budget categories for your new budget lines. Of course, if you're spending money to eat out, you can simply add a row called "Restaurants" to your food category, as long as you keep in mind that purchases are necessary, but drive-thru restaurants or fine-dining restaurants Three-course meals are not.

Step 3: Subtract expenses from income
Math time! (It won't be that bad. But it is absolutely necessary. Let's do this.)

Deduct all your expenses from your income. This number should be zero. We call this zero-based budgeting.

Here's the key: zero-based budgeting doesn't mean letting your bank account go to zero. Leave a little margin there of around $100 to $300.

It also doesn't mean you're wasting all your money. And here's why we love this method. Zero-based budgeting simply means that you give every dollar a purpose: spending, giving, saving, or paying off debt. Everything is taken into account and given a purpose.

You work hard for your money, right? Well, it should work hard for you! Each a single dollar.

Okay, but what do you do when you subtract your expenses from your income and you're left with money? Don't leave it there. You end up mindlessly spending it on coffee, supermarket sweets, and one-click deals of the day. Put those dollars to work by putting "extra" money toward your current monetary goal.

All you have to do is reduce spending until your income minus expenses is zero. (Note:

Start with the budget lines for dining out and entertainment. If restaurants are your language of choice, this will be a blow. Don't spend more than you earn

If you're still struggling to make ends meet, don't forget the power of a side job or overtime. Remember not to increase your expenses as your income increases. Your extra money should cover your planned expenses.

Does math stress you out a little? Listen, let EveryDollar do it for you. Our free budgeting app is designed for this zero-based budgeting task, and you don't need to constantly resort to the calculator to get everything right.

Well, that's it for creating the budget. The next two steps are to persevere.

Step 4: Track your expenses (throughout the month)

Are you ready to learn one of the biggest secrets to budgeting and doing it very, very well? Good, because we don't want to keep it a secret. Here it is: Track your transactions.

Publishing the plan on paper, in your spreadsheet, or in your app is just a lot of good intentions without this step. It's like writing down your goal to run a marathon, creating a training plan, lacing up your shoes, and plopping down on the couch with a bag of donuts.

What are we talking about? When tracking your transactions, you should record everything that happens with your money throughout the month.

When you fill up the gas tank, deduct this cost from the transportation cost. When you pay rent, deduct these costs from your housing costs. If you buy a coffee on the way to the office, deduct that expense from your personal expenses (or from the budget line you established for perks that help you at work).

Track your transactions regularly. This could be at the end of each day or it means making a purchase before leaving the supermarket parking lot. Or it could mean once a week. Everything that works for you and every expense is captured.

Make any necessary adjustments when tracking. Yes really! This is your budget. They make it work for you. If your electric bill is higher than you thought, simply adjust another budget line to compensate. If your water bill turns out to be lower, rejoice and transfer the money to your current monetary goal, or add it to a budget line you've gone over.

We can't say enough about tracking your transactions. In short, we love this budgeting step because it puts you in charge of your budget, yourself, and your money goals. (Even your spouse if you're married! And remember EveryDollar? You both share an account, so you plan as a team!) No secrets. No, pretend there was no purchase.

Don't overspend because when you enter expenses you'll see what's left on each budget line! You will immediately know what is left so you don't overspend.

Keep track of your budget. Your budget is not a set-it-and-forget-it project. It is not a slow cooker. Transaction tracking gives you access to your budget at any time and allows you to make adjustments so you know where your money is going at all times.

Know your spending habits and adjust them so you can get back on track toward your goals and finally make them a reality. A monthly budget each.

Step 5: Create a new budget before the month starts

While your budget shouldn't change much from month to month, the fact is that no two months are exactly the same. That's why you create a new budget every month, before the month begins. Then you can look at specific expenses and say, "That won't be a surprise in my bank account, thank you very much."

When you're ready to start your next budget, simply copy this month's budget to the next and then make changes to anything new that comes up.

Below are some examples of specific monthly expenses to prepare for:

Celebrations like birthdays and anniversaries: never forget them.

Holidays: Need decorations, gifts or a feast?

Seasonal Shopping: Don't forget to budget for back-to-school season, coffee flavor releases in the fall, and your kickball league in the spring.

Semiannual Expenses: Do you pay for your car insurance twice a year? Need an oil change next month?

Annual Expenses: Is it time for your annual eye exam? Do you need to budget for your pet because Sir Barksalot needs to be vaccinated at the vet?

Here's one way to incorporate these changing expenses into your budget:

Create a budget category called Specific Monthly Expenses, Alternate Expenses, or Discretionary (if you like big words).

Then add all the rows you need for this month and delete the ones from last month that you no longer need.

Where does the money come from? You can reduce spending elsewhere and move money to this category. Taking between $5 and $20 from a few budget lines really adds up. Literally or if possible, increase your monthly income. (It's time for some extra freelancing!)

Hey, if this part sounds complicated or clumsy to you, it's because it may be at the beginning. It takes about three months for people to really master budgeting, so be patient and keep working at it! The benefits of budgeting will far outweigh the hassles.

Chapter six

How to track your expenses

If you want to win with money, you must change your actions with money. You can do this by setting a budget and sticking to it. And you can do this by tracking your expenses.

This is the secret to taking your budget from good intentions to great results. Let's talk about how to track your expenses in four steps and why it's so important.

Steps to track your expenses
Tracking your spending (i.e. keeping track of your transactions) isn't difficult, it's a habit. And like other important habits you know, like flossing it takes some work and repetition to go from trying to remember to

doing it naturally. But you will. And your teeth and your budget will thank you. Simply follow these four steps.

Step one: create a budget
Without this, you won't be able to track your expenses. What is a budget? It's your monthly money plan where you assign a purpose to every dollar you bring in during the month, whether it's to spend, save, or donate.

And listen, budgets get a bad rap. Has anyone ever told you that a budget is too limited? The truth is that the budget does not control you, you control it. It's a guide you create to make sure your money does what you tell it to do. So it actually gives you permission to spend money!
And this is how you create a budget:

1. List your income.

List all paychecks that arrive this month. (Don't forget extras like that part-time job!) Add it all up. This is the amount of money you need to have available this month!

Do you have irregular income? Just look at what he's done in the last few months. Enter the lowest amount as your planned income for this month. We'll talk more about this in a moment.

2. List your expenses.

It's time to plan everything you will pay this month. List your expenses in this order:

Donations (10% of your income)
Savings (depending on your Baby Step)
Four walls (food, supplies, shelter/lodging and transportation)
Other essentials (insurance, debt, child care, etc.)
Extras (entertainment, restaurants, etc.)

3. Remove your expenses from your income.

This should be zero. If there is still extra money left, great! Put it on your current Baby Step (the guided, proven path to saving, paying off debt, and building wealth). If you have a negative number, reduce the planned totals or eliminate the extras until you get zero.

This is called zero-based budgeting, and like we said, it's about using every dollar you make to get the job done. That way, he'll work as hard as you do.

Now that you've set your budget, you need to stay on track. This is where tracking comes in!

Step Two: When You Make Money, Track It
When your regular paycheck arrives, record it in the income portion of your

budget. If you make money part-time or sell something, sign up too!

This step is especially important if you have irregular income. Remember that you planned low when declaring your income. If your income turns out to be higher than planned, now is the time to adapt.

Even if you have a regular income: stick to it! On the one hand, you can ensure that there are no problems with your paycheck. On the other hand, it's another way to stick to your budget (which is always a definite win).

Step Three: When You Spend Money, Track It
Track every expense you make. The whole month.

When you fill up the gas tank, deduct this cost from your transportation budget line. When you pay rent, deduct these costs from

your housing bill. When you buy tickets to
your favorite boy band's reunion tour,
deduct that entertainment cost.

You get the picture. When money leaves
your wallet, checking account, PayPal
account, cash envelope, purse, or old piggy
bank, keep track.

When tracking, be sure to subtract as well.
This will help you know how much
left in your different budget categories.
This is where the magic happens, because
this is where you control your spending so
you don't overspend!

Step Four: Establish a Regular Pacing of
Follow-Up
Track your expenses regularly. This could
be once a week or at the end of each day,
or before you leave the supermarket parking
lot.

Whatever works for you and keeps track of every expense without losing paper receipts in the kitchen drawer, which should be some kind of portal to another world. (How else do you explain things that go in but never come out?)

If you're married, make sure you're both working with the same budget and keeping track of expenses. This is great for accountability and communication. That way, neither of you will ever say, "I didn't know you spent most of your entertainment budget on zipline tickets." "I wanted to sign us up for a hip-hop dance class for couples."

•Why should you track your expenses?
We just touched on this, but now let's go deeper. Because let's face it: If all you do is write down your planned budget lines at the beginning of each month, you're not responsible for sticking to those lines.

Many of us start "budgeting" this way. And it's a start. It's good to have an idea of what money should go where. But if you don't track your spending, you won't know where your money is really going. You run the risk of constantly setting unrealistic budgets and never reaching your financial goals.

And that's not what we want for you. We want you to be successful. Ten times! So let's look at different methods to achieve this.

Four ways to track your expenses
1. Pencil and paper
Don't discard old school methods. Many people stick to a paper budget as a method of keeping track of money.

Advantage: The biggest advantage here (aside from not requiring access to technology) is that physically writing things down requires an active brain. And an active mind is really helpful when it comes to money.

Disadvantage: The disadvantage of this method is obvious: most of us can't keep up with paper copies of things these days. Sometimes you misplace receipts (or lose them in your kitchen drawer). Or forget about the money you spent on a quick trip to the dollar store. Or don't write down some debit card purchases.

Any of these communication breakdowns (with yourself or your spouse) can result in a ruined budget.

Conclusion: Hey, making a budget with pen and paper is much better than having no budget at all. If it's the only path you want to follow, do it! Also, if you want to start with a paper budget and then move on to another method, check out our quick start budget.

2. Envelope system

The envelope system focuses on paying cash for as many things as possible within the budget. You can issue things like pensions, mortgages and some utilities automatically and for other bills you can send checks or make a debit card payment online. However, for all expenses you pay personally, you must pay in cash.

At the beginning of the month, put cash in envelopes (or use a special divided wallet) labeled with your budget lines. Food, entertainment and restaurants are three great examples.

Advantage: By using the envelope system as a method of tracking expenses, you will know exactly when to cut back on your spending because you can see when the envelope is running out. And when the envelope is empty, you're done spending. Basically, your money tracks itself.

Disadvantage: Let's face it, paying cash can sometimes be inconvenient. Additionally, with the rise of e-commerce, paying cash is not always an option.

Bottom line: While there are downsides, this is a powerful way to track spending because physically seeing the money come out of the envelope brings a whole new level of responsibility. Even if you choose a different method to track your expenses, using the envelope system for some of your budget lines is a good way to manage your money.

3. Computer spreadsheets
It's time to talk about digitalization: computer spreadsheets as a method of tracking costs.

Benefit: Many people are fans of spreadsheets and will tell you about the benefits until the end of time. Tons of templates, the ability to customize your budget, the beauty of having the calculations done for you on screen these are just a few of the benefits of spreadsheet budgets.

Disadvantage: One problem with this method is that these spreadsheet enthusiasts are not always married to other spreadsheet enthusiasts. Couples should communicate openly about their expenses. Don't let spreadsheets get in the way of your happy ending!

The second disadvantage of spreadsheets is that you have to physically go to your computer to keep up with your expenses. If you don't check in regularly to enter expenses, your budget isn't really a budget, it's just a spreadsheet full of plans. You start by developing the plan, but plans without implementation do not achieve the objectives.

Bottom line: Again, if spreadsheets are the only way to manage your budget and track your expenses, that's better than skipping budgeting altogether!

And here's the thing: computer spreadsheets aren't the worst or anything. But do you know what is always by your side? Your phone. This brings us to the next, and dare we say boldest, option for tracking your spending. Drum roll please.

4. Budget Apps
Especially EveryDollar. We don't mess around here. You can create a budget on the go and literally transform your financial life.

Advantage: You can log in on your phone and track expenses as they appear in your bank account. Don't leave the dollar store parking lot without noticing that you spent $3 plus tax on a birthday balloon, a gift bag, and a stuffed clownfish that you hope your little niece thinks is Nemo.

As you can see, the convenience of a budgeting app is its biggest advantage. Of course, EveryDollar offers even more. Customize your templates to fit your spending and saving needs. Set up funds to achieve big monetary goals. And you can turn two budgets into one with your spouse by syncing both devices with an EveryDollar account.
And remember: upgrading to the premium version of EveryDollar will automatically put your expenses directly into your budget. No receipt memory. No calculation error. No secret expenses. This brings ease, precision and accountability to your budget planning.

Disadvantage: The most important thing to remember is this: you can't set your budget and then leave it as is (but that goes for any budgeting method). The app won't freeze your bank account if you want to buy a 17-layer burrito that will ruin your restaurant budget. The only downside to a budgeting app is that you still have to get used to tracking these expenses.

Conclusion: If you don't pay attention to where your money goes, you will always wonder where it went. But if you arm yourself with the right tool (aka EveryDollar, our favorite spending tracker) and know that the work is worth it (which we can attest to from our own experience), you'll go beyond good intentions to achieve financial success.

Get an expense tracker and track your expenses (every single one of them)

OK. You've learned the why and how, as well as popular methods for tracking money. Now is the time to start. Download EveryDollar and easily get into the habit of tracking your expenses (every single one of them).

Come on! This is the secret to making a good budget. And now that it's no longer a secret, you can make it happen!

Chapter seven

What is a personal finance assessment?

"We should do a financial audit" is usually one of the first things you hear from a financial advisor. Words like "valuation" and "finances" can cause stress and confusion for some people. But it's not as complex as you think. A review of your finances is a valuable process that can help you increase accuracy and achieve a better outcome for your financial plan.

•Conducting a financial audit
A financial audit is a comprehensive examination of your financial expenses. The goal of a financial audit is to ensure that your spending habits do not pose a threat to your financial well-being. Although some

people focus on the negative aspect of the word "review," the truth is that it is an essential part of any financial planning process. It is important to know all areas of your finances in order to make an appropriate plan. Without taking a look at some of the nastier aspects of your finances, your report may not be able to fully help you.

Without a thorough financial audit, neither you nor your financial advisor will be able to know your monthly income and expenses. Without this information, creating a financial plan is difficult and the chances of success are lower.

•What exactly is being checked?
The financial review process is often more like an interview than a review and consists of several steps. An experienced financial advisor will tell you exactly what he needs from you. Let's take a look at some of the

steps that will likely be part of your evaluation:

Income

The advisor you hire to plan your future financial life should know what your monthly income is and where that income comes from. Just as a car requires fuel to move, a financial plan requires funds to be successful. Therefore, a detailed analysis of the fund is very important. If your financial advisor knows where you spend your money and how much you earn each month, they can help you adjust your budget to maximize efficiency.

Retirement provision

A financial audit will only be successful if your advisor knows how much you are saving for retirement and what your goals are. Not everyone has the same retirement plan. Therefore, providing your advisor with some details will help you better understand your long-term financial goals. You can then optimize your retirement plans or create a new plan that better suits your needs.

Investments

Are you sure your investments are performing optimally? If you haven't received a financial report yet, you can't be sure of the answer. Sometimes we are lucky enough to invest in assets that give us great returns, but this is not always the case. Sharing the details of your investment portfolio with your advisor is an important step toward a solid, well-thought-out financial plan. Let your advisor know if you are happy with your investments or if you would like to change your portfolio mix.

Insurance

Are your loved ones protected if the worst happens to you? Life is unpredictable. You should have coverage to make sure you plan for a potential health problem that prevents you from making money. You should also think about what plans you have if you die unexpectedly. Insurance policies are an important part of a financial review and your financial advisor should know which policies will fit into a new financial plan and which need to be modified to fit your budget needs.

Rebalance your plans

The environment around you, your financial goals, your disposable income or even your dreams can change throughout your life. This means that a financial plan created years ago may not be the best one for you today. Of course, the worst case scenario would be that there is no financial plan at all. A financial review gives you the opportunity to check whether you are still on track or whether your goals need to be adjusted to reflect your current situation.

Conducting a financial audit with the help of a qualified and experienced financial advisor gives you the opportunity to understand your financial options and

discover how you can take advantage of
them.

www.ingramcontent.com/pod-product-compliance
Lightning Source LLC
Chambersburg PA
CBHW050046260726
48658CB00005B/1791